Spotter's Guide to
TREES
of North America

⟨√ **W9-AZR-508**

Alan Mitchell

Special Consultant:
Michael A. Ruggiero
Horticultural specialist
New York Botanical Garden

Illustrated by
Peter Stebbing and Annabel Milne
with additional illustrations by Will Giles

Flowering Dogwood

MAYFLOWER BOOKS
NEW YORK

Contents

Edited by
Sue Jacquemier, Karen Goaman
and Alice Geffen

Manufactured in Spain by Printer, industria
gráfica sa Sant Vicenç dels Horts, Barcelona
D.L. 14.139-1979

**Library of Congress Cataloging
in Publication Data**

Mitchell, Alan S.
    Spotter's guide to trees
of North America.

    Includes index.
    1. Trees – North America – Identification.
I. Title.
Qk481.M67   582'.1609'7   79-738
ISBN 0-8317-8818-6
ISBN 0-8317-8819-4 pbk.

First American Edition

The editors wish to thank the
Brooklyn Botanic Garden for their help.

How to use this book

This book is an identification guide to some of the trees of North America. Take it with you when you go out looking for trees. Not all of these trees will be common in your area, but many may be found in large gardens or parks. (See page 56 for a list of places to visit.)

The book is arranged with conifers first, followed by palm trees, followed by broadleaved trees. Trees that are closely related, for example all the oaks, are grouped together.

The illustrations show important features that will help you to identify a tree at any time of the year. For most of the trees, the leaf, the bark, the shape of a tree in full leaf and its shape in winter (if the tree is deciduous) are shown. Flowers and fruits (including cones) are also sometimes illustrated if they will help you to identify the tree.

The description next to each illustration gives you additional information to help you identify trees.

Remember that there are many clues to help you to recognize a tree, so look carefully at the bark, the tree's shape and other features.

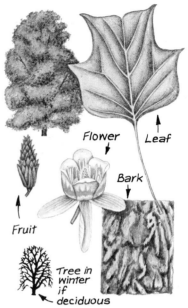

Flower

Leaf

Bark

Fruit

Tree in winter if deciduous

Beside the description is a small blank circle. Each time you spot a new tree, check it off in the circle.

Where each tree grows

At the end of the description of each tree there is a key showing the areas of North America in which the tree grows. The key refers to the following areas:

NE: Northeast   NW: Northwest
SE: Southeast   SW: Southwest
C: Central

Look at the map on page 57 to find out which area you are in.

Scorecard

There is a scorecard on pages 57-62 which gives you a separate score for each tree shown in the book, according to the area in which you see the tree. There is a separate page of scores for each of the areas.

You can also use the scorecard to find out how common a tree is in your area: a common tree scores 5 and a very rare one scores 25.

Parts of a tree

A tree is a plant that grows on a single, central woody stem. A shrub is usually smaller and has many stems.

Trees are divided into two main groups: **conifers** and **broadleaved trees.** Most broadleaved trees have broad flat leaves (which they drop in winter) and they have seeds which are enclosed in fruits (nuts or other forms). Most conifers have narrow, needlelike or scaly leaves. Their fruits are usually woody cones.

Most broadleaved trees are **deciduous** which means that they lose their leaves in the fall and grow new ones again in the spring. Most conifers are **evergreen,** meaning that they keep their green leaves throughout the winter.

These pictures show the different parts of a tree and explain some of the words that appear in the book.

Leaves

There are many different shapes of leaves. Some of the most common ones are shown here.

A leaf that is in one piece is called **simple.**

A leaf that is made up of many **leaflets** is called **compound.**

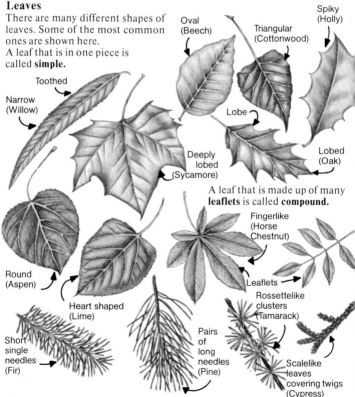

Oval (Beech)

Triangular (Cottonwood)

Spiky (Holly)

Toothed

Narrow (Willow)

Lobe

Deeply lobed (Sycamore)

Lobed (Oak)

Fingerlike (Horse Chestnut)

Round (Aspen)

Heart shaped (Lime)

Leaflets

Rossettelike clusters (Tamarack)

Short single needles (Fir)

Pairs of long needles (Pine)

Scalelike leaves covering twigs (Cypress)

4

Flowers

All trees have flowers that develop into fruits. Here are some different types of flowers.

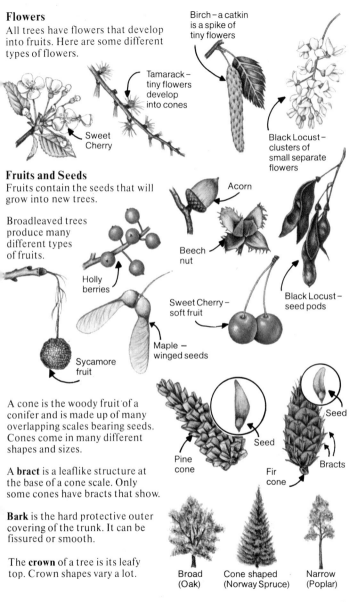

Birch – a catkin is a spike of tiny flowers

Tamarack – tiny flowers develop into cones

Sweet Cherry

Black Locust – clusters of small separate flowers

Fruits and Seeds

Fruits contain the seeds that will grow into new trees.

Broadleaved trees produce many different types of fruits.

Holly berries

Acorn

Beech nut

Sweet Cherry – soft fruit

Black Locust – seed pods

Sycamore fruit

Maple – winged seeds

A cone is the woody fruit of a conifer and is made up of many overlapping scales bearing seeds. Cones come in many different shapes and sizes.

A **bract** is a leaflike structure at the base of a cone scale. Only some cones have bracts that show.

Bark is the hard protective outer covering of the trunk. It can be fissured or smooth.

The **crown** of a tree is its leafy top. Crown shapes vary a lot.

Pine cone

Seed

Fir cone

Seed

Bracts

Broad (Oak)

Cone shaped (Norway Spruce)

Narrow (Poplar)

5

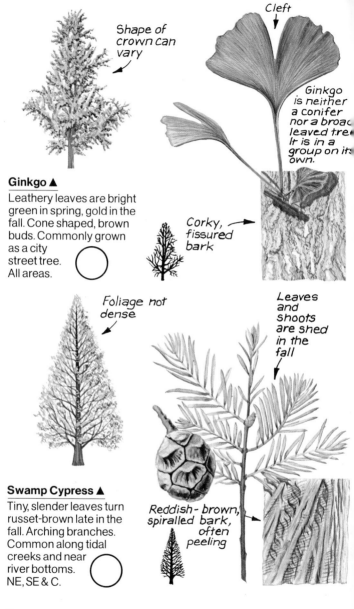

Shape of crown can vary

Cleft

Ginkgo is neither a conifer nor a broad leaved tree. It is in a group on its own.

Ginkgo ▲
Leathery leaves are bright green in spring, gold in the fall. Cone shaped, brown buds. Commonly grown as a city street tree. All areas.

Corky, fissured bark

Foliage not dense

Leaves and shoots are shed in the fall

Swamp Cypress ▲
Tiny, slender leaves turn russet-brown late in the fall. Arching branches. Common along tidal creeks and near river bottoms. NE, SE & C.

Reddish-brown, spiralled bark, often peeling

Trunk swells toward base

Leaves and shoots grow in opposite pairs

Long stalked cones

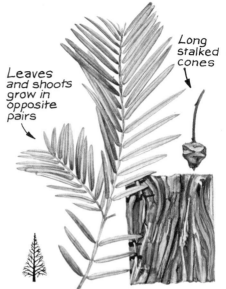

Dawn Redwood ▲

Soft, light green leaves turn red-brown and are shed in the fall. Bark has stringy orange-brown strips. Big gardens, parks. NE, SE & NW.

Shapely, slender crown

Whorls of soft, bright green leaves

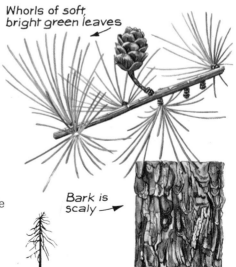

Bark is scaly

Tamarack ▲

Leaves turn yellow in the fall. Small red female flowers appear before leaves, turn purple and then turn into woody cones. NE & C.

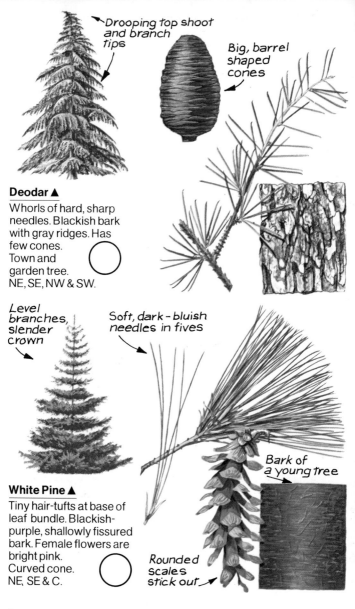

Drooping top shoot and branch tips

Big, barrel shaped cones

Deodar ▲
Whorls of hard, sharp needles. Blackish bark with gray ridges. Has few cones. Town and garden tree. NE, SE, NW & SW.

Level branches, slender crown

Soft, dark-bluish needles in fives

Bark of a young tree

White Pine ▲
Tiny hair-tufts at base of leaf bundle. Blackish-purple, shallowly fissured bark. Female flowers are bright pink. Curved cone. NE, SE & C.

Rounded scales stick out

8

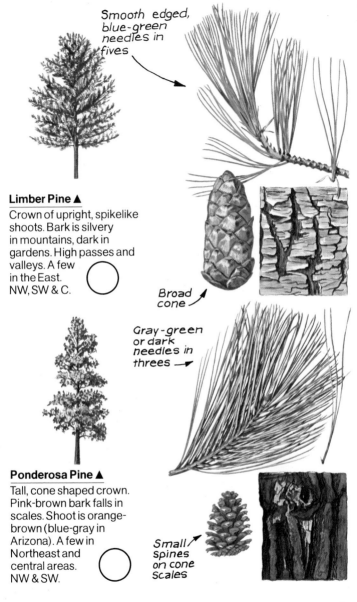

Smooth edged, blue-green needles in fives

Limber Pine ▲

Crown of upright, spikelike shoots. Bark is silvery in mountains, dark in gardens. High passes and valleys. A few in the East. NW, SW & C.

Broad cone

Gray-green or dark needles in threes →

Ponderosa Pine ▲

Tall, cone shaped crown. Pink-brown bark falls in scales. Shoot is orange-brown (blue-gray in Arizona). A few in Northeast and central areas. NW & SW.

Small spines on cone scales

9

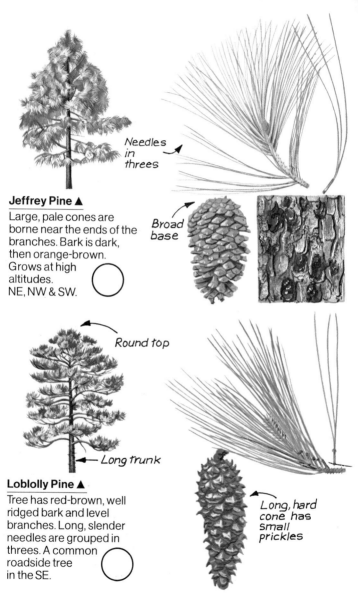

Jeffrey Pine ▲

Large, pale cones are borne near the ends of the branches. Bark is dark, then orange-brown. Grows at high altitudes. NE, NW & SW.

Needles in threes

Broad base

Round top

Long trunk

Loblolly Pine ▲

Tree has red-brown, well ridged bark and level branches. Long, slender needles are grouped in threes. A common roadside tree in the SE.

Long, hard cone has small prickles

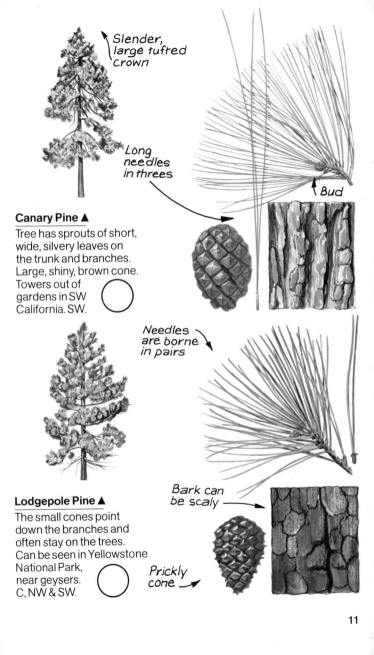

Slender, large tufted crown

Long needles in threes

↳ Bud

Canary Pine ▲

Tree has sprouts of short, wide, silvery leaves on the trunk and branches. Large, shiny, brown cone. Towers out of gardens in SW California. SW.

Needles are borne in pairs

Lodgepole Pine ▲

The small cones point down the branches and often stay on the trees. Can be seen in Yellowstone National Park, near geysers. C, NW & SW.

Bark can be scaly

Prickly cone

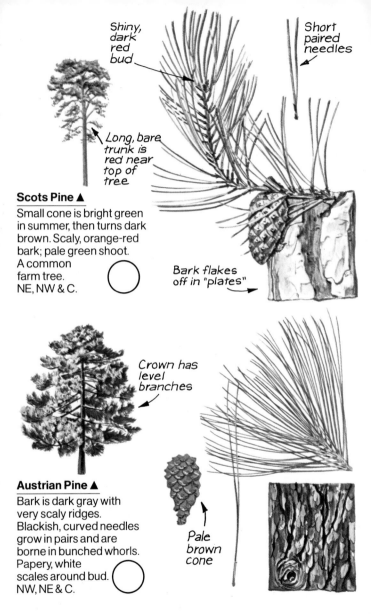

Shiny, dark red bud

Short paired needles

Long, bare trunk is red near top of tree

Scots Pine ▲

Small cone is bright green in summer, then turns dark brown. Scaly, orange-red bark; pale green shoot. A common farm tree. NE, NW & C.

Bark flakes off in "plates"

Crown has level branches

Austrian Pine ▲

Bark is dark gray with very scaly ridges. Blackish, curved needles grow in pairs and are borne in bunched whorls. Papery, white scales around bud. NW, NE & C.

Pale brown cone

Paired needles

Young shoot

Aleppo Pine ▲

Broad, light and rather fuzzy crown. Dark orange and gray bark. Common in gardens in Arizona and California. Small round buds. SW.

Shiny, reddish cones stay on tree for years

Single-leaf Nut Pine ▲

A low, bushy tree. Large flat cone has few scales, which open widely. Grows in rocky, arid areas; sometimes planted in borders. SW.

Rounded, stout, sharp needle

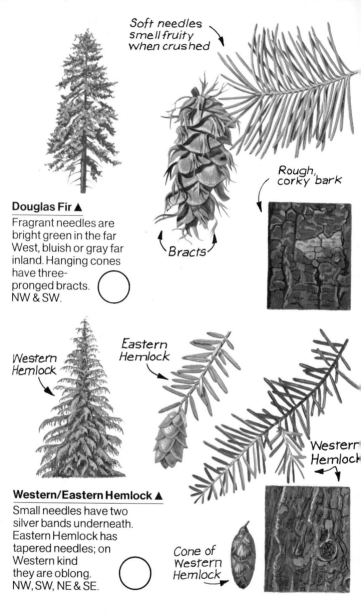

Soft needles smell fruity when crushed

Rough, corky bark

Bracts

Douglas Fir ▲

Fragrant needles are bright green in the far West, bluish or gray far inland. Hanging cones have three-pronged bracts. NW & SW.

Western Hemlock

Eastern Hemlock

Western Hemlock

Western/Eastern Hemlock ▲

Small needles have two silver bands underneath. Eastern Hemlock has tapered needles; on Western they are oblong. NW, SW, NE & SE.

Cone of Western Hemlock

14

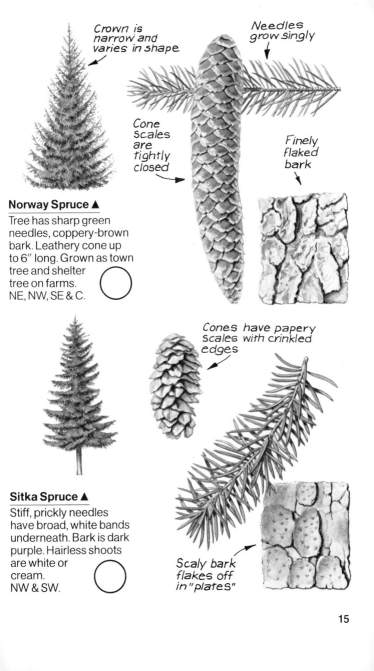

Crown is narrow and varies in shape

Needles grow singly

Cone scales are tightly closed

Finely flaked bark

Norway Spruce ▲
Tree has sharp green needles, coppery-brown bark. Leathery cone up to 6" long. Grown as town tree and shelter tree on farms.
NE, NW, SE & C.

Cones have papery scales with crinkled edges

Sitka Spruce ▲
Stiff, prickly needles have broad, white bands underneath. Bark is dark purple. Hairless shoots are white or cream.
NW & SW.

Scaly bark flakes off in "plates"

15

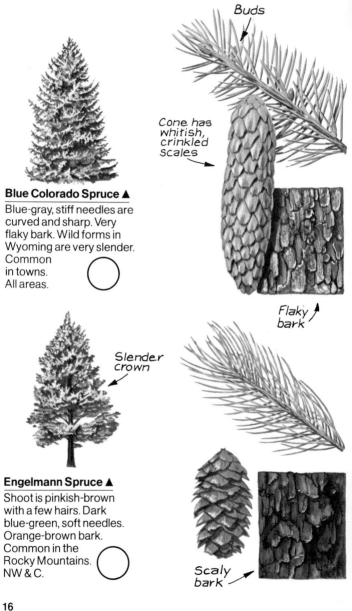

Blue Colorado Spruce ▲
Blue-gray, stiff needles are
curved and sharp. Very
flaky bark. Wild forms in
Wyoming are very slender.
Common
in towns.
All areas.

Buds

Cone has
whitish,
crinkled
scales

Flaky
bark

Slender
crown

Engelmann Spruce ▲
Shoot is pinkish-brown
with a few hairs. Dark
blue-green, soft needles.
Orange-brown bark.
Common in the
Rocky Mountains.
NW & C.

Scaly
bark

16

Foliage hanging from upswept branches

Scalelike hard leaves have aniseed scent

Diamond shaped cone scales wrinkle when they ripen

Giant Sequoia ▲

The huge trunk is swollen towards base which can be 33′ through. Very thick, spongy, dull red-brown bark. May live for 3500 years. NW & SW.

Needles parted on either side of shoot

Coast Redwood ▲

Hard needles have white bands underneath. Gray and orange-red bark. Small, crinkled cone. One of the world's tallest trees. NW & SW.

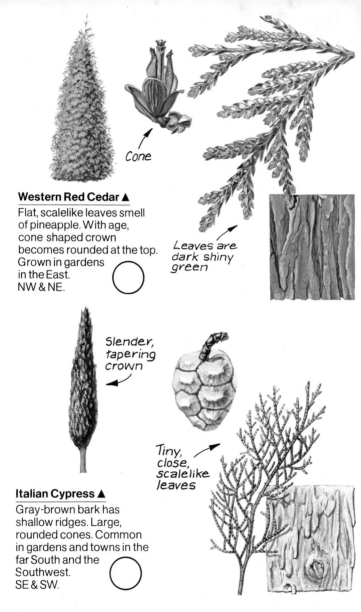

Cone

Western Red Cedar ▲

Flat, scalelike leaves smell of pineapple. With age, cone shaped crown becomes rounded at the top. Grown in gardens in the East.
NW & NE.

Leaves are dark shiny green

Slender, tapering crown

Tiny, close, scalelike leaves

Italian Cypress ▲

Gray-brown bark has shallow ridges. Large, rounded cones. Common in gardens and towns in the far South and the Southwest.
SE & SW.

Buds

Shapely
cone
shaped
crown

Upright
cones
break up
on tree
in the fall

Balsam Fir ▲

Leathery, strap shaped
leaves are borne on each
side of the shoot. Dark,
deeply fissured bark.
Tree smells of
balsam when
handled. NE.

Fruit

Canary Palm ▲

A very sturdy palm with a
huge crown. Bright green,
featherlike leaves curve
downward. Tree bears
large bunches of
pale orange
flowers. SE & SW.

19

Dead
leaves
in long
clusters

Stout
trunk

Leaves
edged
with
threads

California Washingtonia ▲

Tall palm with fan shaped
leaves. Pale orange
flowers are borne in large,
drooping clusters.
Common in southern parts
of Florida and
California.
SE & SW.

Moplike
crown

Young
bark

Old
bark

Fan shaped
leaves

Mexican or Slender
Washingtonia ▲

Slender, slightly wavy
trunk. Narrow lobed
leaves are borne high up.
Common in
southern Florida.
SW & SE.

▲ Cabbage Palmetto

Large, grayish, fan shaped
leaves. Bases of leaf-stalks
interlace on the trunk; stay
after leaves have
fallen. Rare in the
Southwest. SE.

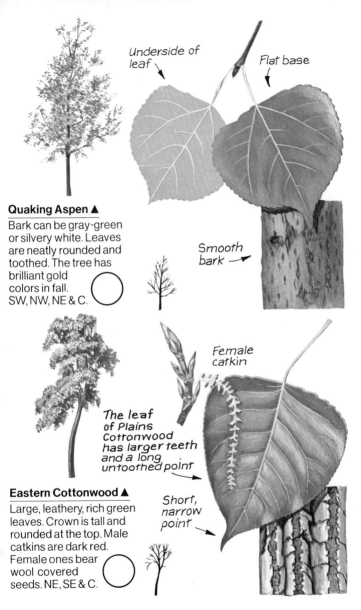

Underside of leaf

Flat base

Quaking Aspen ▲
Bark can be gray-green or silvery white. Leaves are neatly rounded and toothed. The tree has brilliant gold colors in fall. SW, NW, NE & C.

Smooth bark →

Female catkin

The leaf of Plains Cottonwood has larger teeth and a long untoothed point

Eastern Cottonwood ▲
Large, leathery, rich green leaves. Crown is tall and rounded at the top. Male catkins are dark red. Female ones bear wool covered seeds. NE, SE & C.

Short, narrow point

Slender, cone shaped crown

Underside of leaf

Bolle's Poplar/Erect
White Poplar ▲

Shoots and new leaves are thickly covered with short, white hairs. Cream or white bark. Common in the Mid-West. SW & C.

Black marks on smooth bark

Upright, narrow crown

Leaf shape varies

Lombardy Poplar ▲

Red catkins appear before leaves. Tree is bright gold in the fall in the South and West. Narrowly pointed, small leaves. Common. All areas.

Bark has shallow ridges

Paper/Canoe Birch ▲

Large, round-based leaf on hairy stalk. Fruits form from long flower clusters (catkins). Low, wide, branching crown.
NE, NW & C.

Catkin

Silvery-white bark can be speckled black or shaded brown

European White Birch ▲

Small and irregularly toothed leaf is borne on a smooth stalk. Fruits and flowers similar to Paper Birch.
Houses, farms.
NE, NW, SW & C.

Catkin

Silvery bark peels off in ribbons

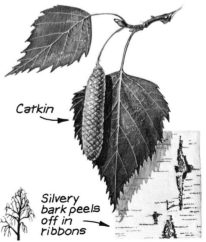

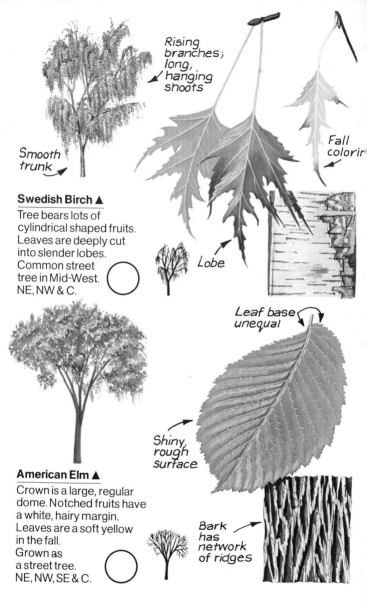

Rising branches; long, hanging shoots

Smooth trunk

Fall coloring

Swedish Birch ▲

Tree bears lots of cylindrical shaped fruits. Leaves are deeply cut into slender lobes. Common street tree in Mid-West. NE, NW & C.

Lobe

Leaf base unequal

Shiny, rough surface

American Elm ▲

Crown is a large, regular dome. Notched fruits have a white, hairy margin. Leaves are a soft yellow in the fall. Grown as a street tree. NE, NW, SE & C.

Bark has network of ridges

Wide, open crown

Leaf is nearly equal at base

Spreading branches

Slender leaf

Siberian/Dwarf Elm ▲
Tree bears circular fruit in dense clusters. Grown as a shelter tree in the Mid-West, and as a shade tree along desert roads. SW, NW, SE & C.

Leaf turning to fall color

Smooth edge

Toothed edge

Sugarberry ▲
Leaf form varies from toothed (northern parts) to smooth (south of Virginia). Small, round berries can be orange, becoming purple. SW, C & SE.

Smooth bark with lumps and ridges

25

Berry

Chinese Tallow Tree ▲
Yellow flowers grow in a long spike. Fruit is a shiny, flattened berry. Leaves are on smooth, long, slender stalks. Shoots are light green.
SE & SW.

Bark is dull yellow-gray or brownish

Upswept crown has lots of slender branches

Bradford Pear ▲
Tree looks pale green from a distance. White flowers appear early. Shiny, olive-brown shoot. Grown as a street tree in New York and other cities. SE & C.

Round base

Dark green fruit speckled buff

Upper branches grow upward

Leaves turn red in fall

Sweet Cherry/Gean ▲

Tree has lots of single white flowers in the spring. Leaves on dark red stalk. Common in British Columbia, New England. NW & NE.

Cherry (not edible)

Horizontal strips on shiny bark

Thick, cone shaped crown

Leaf uneven at base

American Linden ▲

Gray-brown bark is deeply fissured. Sharply toothed leaves are rich green on both sides. Shoot and bud are green. Common street tree. NE, SE, NW & C.

Fruit

27

Rounded at the top

Underside of leaf is pale and hairy

Fruits

Small-leafed European Linden ▲

Small, pale yellow flowers are very fragrant. Shoots are red-brown; buds are dark red. Common street tree in northern USA, southern Canada. NE, SE, NW & C.

Open, widely branched crown

Leaf is hairy beneath

Empress Tree ▲

Bark is gray-brown and smooth. Lilac-blue, trumpet shaped flowers. Very big, floppy leaf is broader in young trees. NE, SE, NW & SW.

Sticky fruit

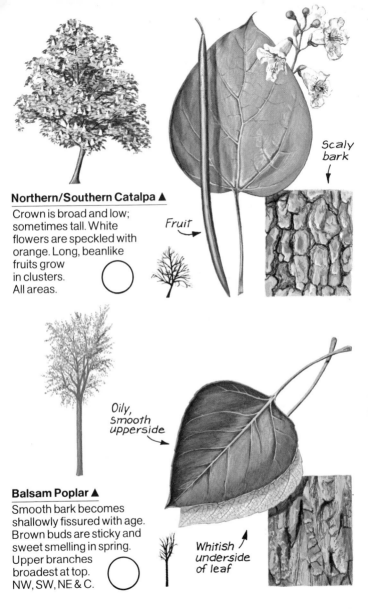

Northern/Southern Catalpa ▲

Crown is broad and low; sometimes tall. White flowers are speckled with orange. Long, beanlike fruits grow in clusters. All areas.

Fruit

Scaly bark

Balsam Poplar ▲

Smooth bark becomes shallowly fissured with age. Brown buds are sticky and sweet smelling in spring. Upper branches broadest at top. NW, SW, NE & C.

Oily, smooth upperside

Whitish underside of leaf

29

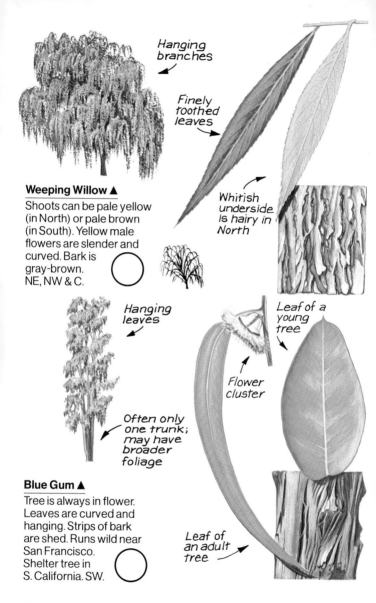

Hanging branches

Finely toothed leaves

Whitish underside is hairy in North

Weeping Willow ▲

Shoots can be pale yellow (in North) or pale brown (in South). Yellow male flowers are slender and curved. Bark is gray-brown. NE, NW & C.

Hanging leaves

Often only one trunk; may have broader foliage

Leaf of a young tree

Flower cluster

Leaf of an adult tree

Blue Gum ▲

Tree is always in flower. Leaves are curved and hanging. Strips of bark are shed. Runs wild near San Francisco. Shelter tree in S. California. SW.

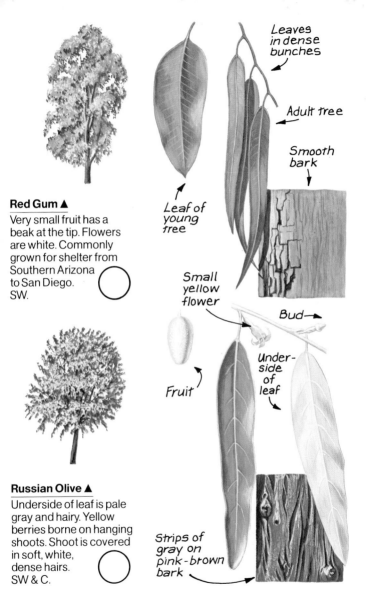

Red Gum ▲

Very small fruit has a beak at the tip. Flowers are white. Commonly grown for shelter from Southern Arizona to San Diego. SW.

Leaves in dense bunches

Adult tree

Smooth bark

Leaf of young tree

Russian Olive ▲

Underside of leaf is pale gray and hairy. Yellow berries borne on hanging shoots. Shoot is covered in soft, white, dense hairs. SW & C.

Small yellow flower

Bud→

Fruit

Under-side of leaf

Strips of gray on pink-brown bark

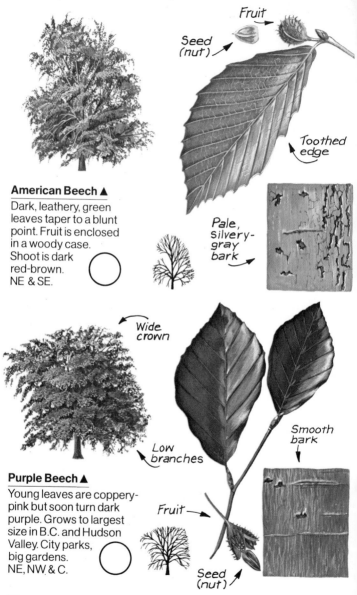

Fruit

Seed
(nut)

Toothed
edge

American Beech ▲
Dark, leathery, green
leaves taper to a blunt
point. Fruit is enclosed
in a woody case.
Shoot is dark
red-brown.
NE & SE.

Pale,
silvery-
gray
bark

Wide
crown

Low
branches

Smooth
bark

Purple Beech ▲
Young leaves are coppery-
pink but soon turn dark
purple. Grows to largest
size in B.C. and Hudson
Valley. City parks,
big gardens.
NE, NW, & C.

Fruit

Seed
(nut)

Blackjack Oak ▲

Rough bark has dark blackish-gray ridges. Crown is broad and low. Broad leaf widens into huge lobes at tip. Common in roadside thickets. SE & C.

Spiny teeth

Fall color of leaves

Acorn

Red Oak ▲

Acorns are very small in the first year, swell in the second year. Dark gray bark has flat ridges between black fissures. NE, NW, SE & C.

33

Fall color is orange or red

White Oak ▲
A broad tree with straight branches. Slightly shaggy, pale gray bark has black fissures. Leaves have very deep, curved lobes. C, SE & NE.

Acorn

Post Oak ▲
Brownish-gray bark is closely fissured. Leaves are pale yellowish-gray on the underside. Shoot is covered in soft, orange-brown hairs. NE, SE & C.

Acorn

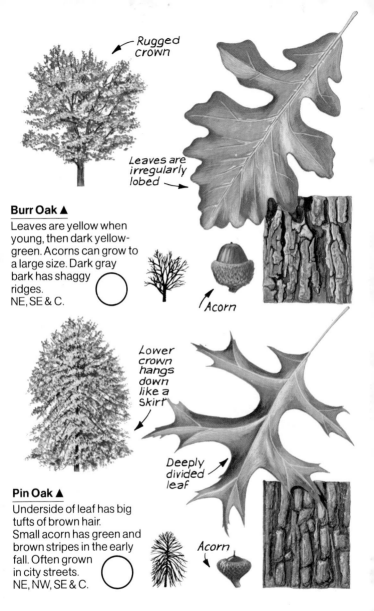

Rugged crown

Leaves are irregularly lobed →

Burr Oak ▲
Leaves are yellow when young, then dark yellow-green. Acorns can grow to a large size. Dark gray bark has shaggy ridges.
NE, SE & C.

Acorn

Lower crown hangs down like a skirt

Deeply divided leaf →

Pin Oak ▲
Underside of leaf has big tufts of brown hair. Small acorn has green and brown stripes in the early fall. Often grown in city streets.
NE, NW, SE & C.

Acorn

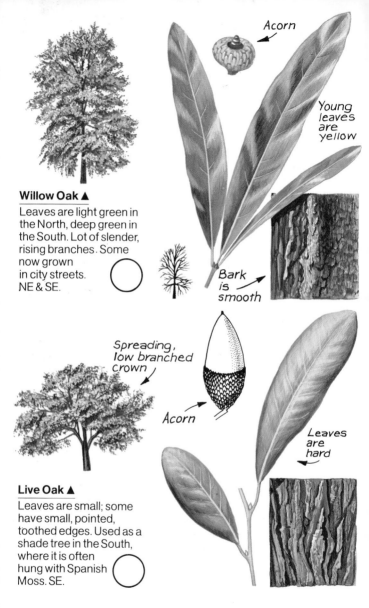

Willow Oak ▲

Leaves are light green in the North, deep green in the South. Lot of slender, rising branches. Some now grown in city streets. NE & SE.

Acorn

Young leaves are yellow

Bark is smooth

Spreading, low branched crown

Acorn

Leaves are hard

Live Oak ▲

Leaves are small; some have small, pointed, toothed edges. Used as a shade tree in the South, where it is often hung with Spanish Moss. SE.

Upright branches at top

Prickly fruit

Sharp teeth

Sweet Gum ▲

Leaves have a sweet fragrance when crushed. Bright green leaves turn brilliant red and crimson in the fall.
Long, slender top.
All areas.

Rough, ridged bark

Big, spreading crown ·

Toothed lobes

Buttonwood/Sycamore ▲

Leaf can be very broad and toothed, or narrower with few teeth. Bark flakes to show cream or bluish-white. New leaves yellow-gray.
SE, NE & C.

Fruit single or in groups of 3 to 5

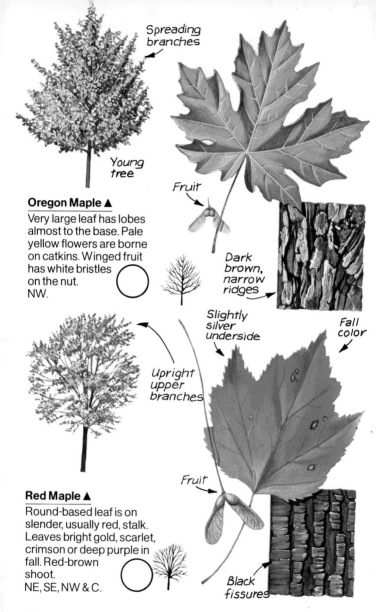

Spreading branches

Young tree

Fruit

Dark brown, narrow ridges

Oregon Maple ▲
Very large leaf has lobes
almost to the base. Pale
yellow flowers are borne
on catkins. Winged fruit
has white bristles
on the nut.
NW.

Slightly silver underside

Fall color

Upright upper branches

Fruit

Red Maple ▲
Round-based leaf is on
slender, usually red, stalk.
Leaves bright gold, scarlet,
crimson or deep purple in
fall. Red-brown
shoot.
NE, SE, NW & C.

Black fissures

Under-side of leaf is silvery

Silver Maple ▲
Unusual crown has long, upright branches at top. Sprouts appear on the tree trunk. Scaly, shaggy bark is dark gray.
All areas.

Winged fruit

Lobes have blunt teeth

Winged fruit

Sugar Maple ▲
Leaves are very bright orange to scarlet in the fall. Shoots are green and smooth. Commonly grown along town roadsides in NE.
NW, NE, SE & C.

Shaggy bark

Whisker tipped teeth

Leaves turn yellow in fall

Norway Maple ▲

Flowers appear in yellow bunches. Bark is gray or brown and finely ridged. Grown as a street tree in northern cities.
NW, NE, SE, C.

Fruits spin as they fall

Large, fragrant flower

Southern Magnolia ▲

Hard leaves can be orange or hairy underneath. Big, upright fruit is gray, then brilliant pink. Broad crown is rounded in North, taller in South. SE, SW & C.

Bark is black, then gray-pink

Cone like fruit

Trunk sometimes very much longer

Ridged bark

Tulip Tree ▲
Old trees have big branches borne high on a clear trunk. Upright fruit stays on tree in winter. Greenish-yellow flower.
NE, SE, NW & SW.

Long outer shoots arch down

White fruit turns pink and red

White Mulberry ▲
Leaves on flowering branches are small, oval, and shiny dark green. Bark is gray with shallow brown fissures.
All areas.

41

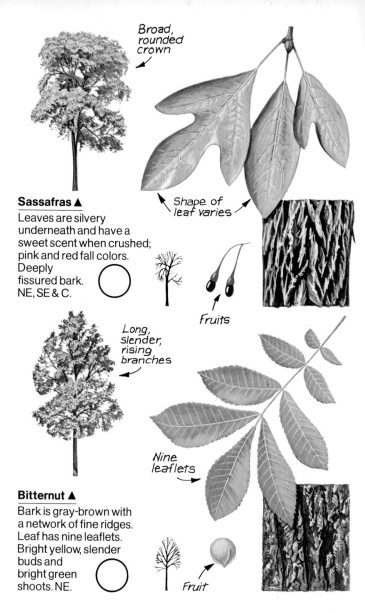

Broad, rounded crown

Shape of leaf varies

Sassafras ▲
Leaves are silvery underneath and have a sweet scent when crushed; pink and red fall colors. Deeply fissured bark. NE, SE & C.

Fruits

Long, slender, rising branches

Nine leaflets

Bitternut ▲
Bark is gray-brown with a network of fine ridges. Leaf has nine leaflets. Bright yellow, slender buds and bright green shoots. NE.

Fruit

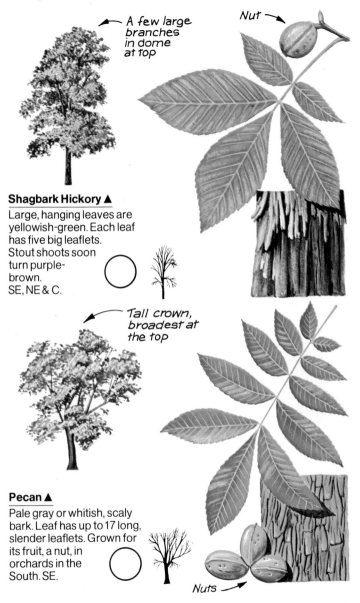

A few large branches in dome at top

Nut →

Shagbark Hickory ▲

Large, hanging leaves are yellowish-green. Each leaf has five big leaflets. Stout shoots soon turn purple-brown.
SE, NE & C.

Tall crown, broadest at the top

Pecan ▲

Pale gray or whitish, scaly bark. Leaf has up to 17 long, slender leaflets. Grown for its fruit, a nut, in orchards in the South. SE.

Nuts →

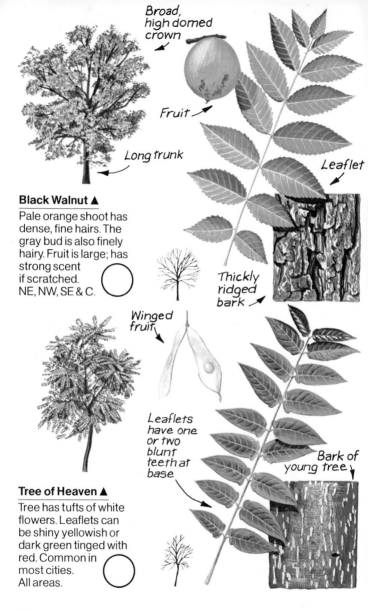

Broad, high domed crown

Fruit

Leaflet

Long trunk

Thickly ridged bark

Black Walnut ▲

Pale orange shoot has dense, fine hairs. The gray bud is also finely hairy. Fruit is large; has strong scent if scratched. NE, NW, SE & C.

Winged fruit

Leaflets have one or two blunt teeth at base

Bark of young tree

Tree of Heaven ▲

Tree has tufts of white flowers. Leaflets can be shiny yellowish or dark green tinged with red. Common in most cities. All areas.

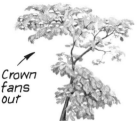

Crown fans out

Mimosa/Silk Tree ▲
Large leaf has hundreds of small leaflets. Rosy-pink flowers are borne in clusters. Smooth shoots are dark green. Town gardens almost everywhere.

Flower

Pagoda Tree ▲
Tree has blue-green shoots. White flowers appear late in spring. Seeds are enclosed in a slender pod. City streets and along boulevards. NE, NW & C.

Leaflet

Broadly ridged bark

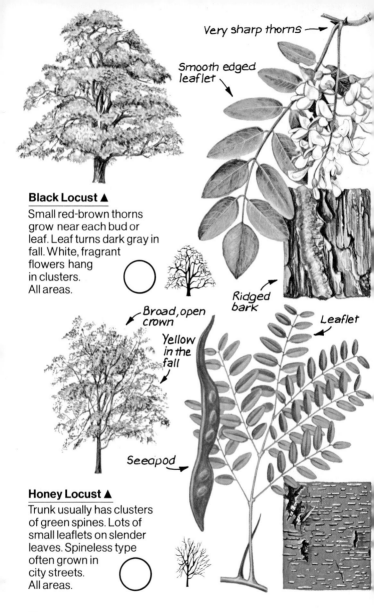

Very sharp thorns →

Smooth edged
leaflet

Black Locust ▲

Small red-brown thorns
grow near each bud or
leaf. Leaf turns dark gray in
fall. White, fragrant
flowers hang
in clusters.
All areas.

Ridged
bark

Broad, open
crown

Yellow
in the
fall

Leaflet

Seedpod

Honey Locust ▲

Trunk usually has clusters
of green spines. Lots of
small leaflets on slender
leaves. Spineless type
often grown in
city streets.
All areas.

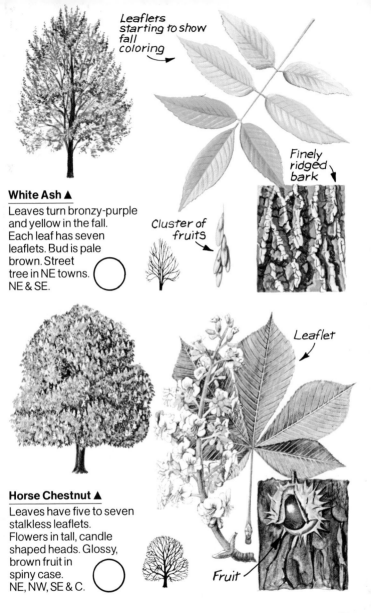

Leaflets starting to show fall coloring

Finely ridged bark

Cluster of fruits

White Ash ▲
Leaves turn bronzy-purple and yellow in the fall. Each leaf has seven leaflets. Bud is pale brown. Street tree in NE towns. NE & SE.

Leaflet

Horse Chestnut ▲
Leaves have five to seven stalkless leaflets. Flowers in tall, candle shaped heads. Glossy, brown fruit in spiny case. NE, NW, SE & C.

Fruit

Growing seedlings

Try growing your own tree from a seed. Pick ripe seeds from trees or from the ground. Acorns (oak seeds) and maple seeds are very easy to find, but almost any fresh seed will do. Most seeds take a couple of months to sprout so be patient.

1

Soak the acorns or other hard nuts overnight in warm water. Take the cups off the acorns, but do not try to remove their shells.

2

Put some stones or pebbles in the bottom of a flower pot. This will help the water to drain properly. Fill the pot with soil or compost until the pot is almost full. Place a saucer under the pot and water the soil well.

3

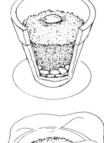

Because the seeds need plenty of room to grow, place only one seed in each pot that you have prepared. Cover the seed with a thin layer of soil. Tamp the soil down to make it firm. Water the soil again lightly.

4

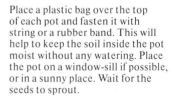

Place a plastic bag over the top of each pot and fasten it with string or a rubber band. This will help to keep the soil inside the pot moist without any watering. Place the pot on a window-sill if possible, or in a sunny place. Wait for the seeds to sprout.

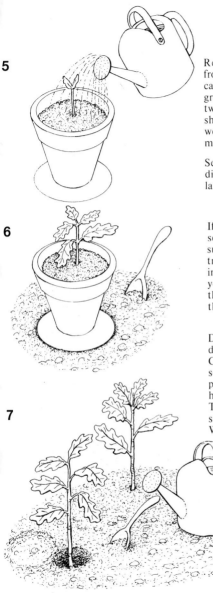

5

Remove the plastic bags from the pots as soon as you can see the seedlings growing. Water the seedlings twice a week. The soil should be damp, but not too wet or else the seedlings may rot.

Seedling leaves often look different from the tree's later leaves.

6

If you can, place your seedlings outside in the summer. In the fall, you can transplant the seedlings into the ground. However, if you prefer, you can leave them in pots inside throughout the winter.

Dig holes which are a bit deeper than the pots. Carefully remove the seedlings and the soil from the pots. Place them in the holes, fill them in with soil. Tamp the soil around the seedling to make it firm. Water it.

7

Winter buds

Most broadleaved trees are deciduous and have no leaves in the winter,
but you can identify them by their
bark and their winter buds. Conifers
have winter buds too, but, since
most conifers are evergreen, their
needles often hide the buds, making
them hard to spot.

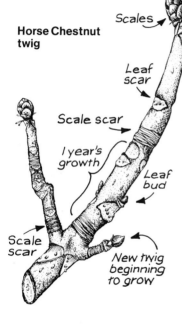

Terminal bud

Terminal bud

Scales

Horse Chestnut twig

Spruce twig

Last year's buds were here

Leaf scar

Scale scar

1 year's growth

Leaf bud

Scale scar

New twig beginning to grow

Winter buds contain the beginnings
of next year's twig, leaves, and
flowers. The buds are protected
from the winter weather by thick,
overlapping scales or by fur. A twig
has several buds. All of these buds
will become twigs and eventually
branches. The terminal (leading)
bud contains the shoot that will
grow the most; the other buds grow
out sideways and are reserves in
case the terminal bud is damaged.
Each year's growth comes from a
bud and ends by making a new bud
at the end of the growing season.

If you look at several different
trees, you will see that there are
many different types of winter buds
(see opposite).

How to tell the age of a twig

You can tell how old a twig is by
examing the scars left by the buds
of previous years. The scales of the
terminal bud leave scars that look
like tight, tiny rings. The distance
between each group of rings shows
how much the twig has grown in a
given year. If you trace back three or
four years, you may notice that in
some years the tree grew more than
others. This is due, in part, to chang-
ing weather conditions and to the
amount of water and food the tree
had.

Identifying winter buds

Here are the winter buds of some trees which you may see.

Red Oak
Pointed, large, dark brown bud on dark brown shoot, often ribbed.

Buttonwood
Small, brown bud hidden until leaf falls; shoot soon turns shiny brown.

White Pine
Pointed orange-brown buds on bright green shoot.

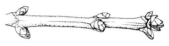

Sugar Maple
Rounded, sharp tipped, scaly bud, dark and pale brown on olive to red-brown shoot.

Paper Birch
Slender, green and brown buds on warty, dark brown shoot.

Black Walnut
Squat, pale brown bud with dense gray hairs on pale brown to orange shoot.

American Elm
Sharp, chestnut-brown bud on light brown shoot.

American Linden
Smooth, bright green, rounded bud on smooth, bright green shoot.

Mimosa
Minute, dark brown bud; dark green, finely ridged shoot with raised warts.

Weeping Willow
Pink to dark red bud has curved tip; shoot is light brown or pale yellow.

Horse Chestnut
Large, red-brown bud glistening with gummy resin on stout, pink-brown shoot.

Reading tree stumps

Just as twigs and branches reflect the growth of a tree, so does the tree's trunk. You can learn a lot about the life of a tree by reading its "calendar" of annual rings. Every year, a tree grows a ring of new wood. You can see these rings on a freshly cut stump. By counting them you can find out how old the tree is. Some trees, like the Giant Sequoia in California, are thousands of years old. If you know when the tree was cut, you can figure out the year it began to grow or how old it was when you were born. This will only work if the tree was cut near the ground. If it was cut too far above the ground, the earliest rings will not be visible.

Stumps that have been cut recently are the easiest to read. But if you find an old stump, you can rub the top with some sandpaper to make the rings show up more clearly. If you want to make a permanent record of the tree's history, put a strip of white paper on the stump going from the bark into the middle. Then rub lightly with a soft pencil or crayon. The rings will show up on the paper as dark lines.

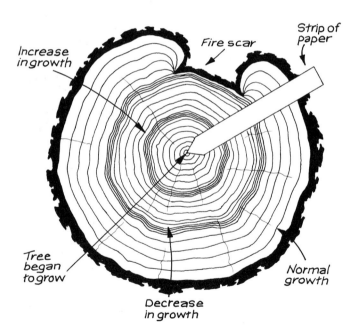

Increase in growth

Fire scar

Strip of paper

Tree began to grow

Normal growth

Decrease in growth

Bark

Trees can also be identified by their bark. The Ponderosa Pine's bark is plated; the American Beech has smooth bark that is grayish; the Shagbark Hickory's bark is shaggy; and the Paper Birch tree has whitish, papery bark that comes off in strips. It is from the Paper Birch that the North American Indians made their famous birch bark canoes.

Ponderosa Pine (plated) | **American Beech (smooth)** | **Shagbark Hickory (shaggy)** | **Paper Birch (papery)**

Bark works like skin. It insulates the tree from heat and cold; and it protects the tree from disease. It also keeps the tree from drying out. Underneath the bark are tubes that carry food (sap) up and down the tree. These tubes can be damaged if the bark is stripped off. If this happens, the tree may die.

Often the bark of a young tree looks different from that of a mature tree. This is because as a tree grows its bark thickens.

How bark patterns are formed

The old bark splits and new bark forms underneath ➔

Making bark rubbings

Making bark rubbings is quite simple. Just tape a piece of thin, strong paper (white or light-colored) to the tree trunk. Then rub firmly up and down with a soft pencil or crayon until the pattern appears. Be careful not to tear the paper by rubbing too hard.

Pressing leaves

You can make a collection of the leaves you find. To press the leaves, put each one between two sheets of soft, absorbent paper (newspaper or blotting paper would be the best). Then put the sheets under a very heavy book and weight it down some more with something very heavy, like a brick. Don't stack up too many sheets – only about three or four per pile.

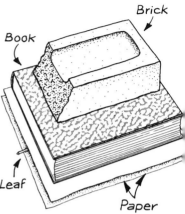

After about a week, when the leaves are flat and dry, you can remove them from the press and paste them in a notebook. Or you can use them for various arts and crafts projects, like a collage, for instance, made with a combination of pressed leaves and other natural objects (grasses, dried seeds, ferns, and so on).

The Shape of Trees

Trees all have different shapes. Some are tall and thin, like the Norway Spruce, and others are vase-shaped like the American Elm. A tree can be identified, in part, by its shape and by the way the branches grow out from its trunk. It is the arrangement of the branches that gives a tree its shape. Winter is a good time to see these shapes.

Other conditions also shape trees, for example the weather. If there is a steady wind in one direction, it can make a tree grow one-sided. If several trees are growing very close together, in a dense forest for example, they will grow quite tall and not branch out till near the top. If a tree grows by itself, it will form a wide crown so that the leaves get plenty of sunlight. People prune trees to get them to grow in special ways.

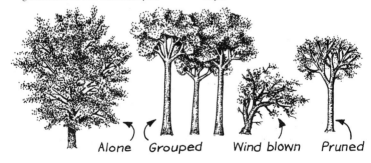

Alone   Grouped   Wind blown   Pruned

Making an album

Why not keep a notebook of trees? You can make a page or more for each tree you spot. Include *when* (the date) you saw the tree and *where* - was it along a road, in the mountains, in a city park, in a field, or in a dense forest? Draw a *picture* of it (or take a photo) to show its shape and the way it grows; paste in a pressed *leaf* (or needle). You can also add a twig showing the tree's winter bud and a bark rubbing that you have made. In the spring you can put in a drawing of the tree's flower and later, in the fall, add one of the fruits or seeds.

If the trees in your album are trees that are near your home, you can keep track of them throughout the year and record their seasonal changes - such as when the flowers bloom and when the leaves begin to change color and fall. You can also keep track of them from year to year. Ask yourself questions. Do the leaves turn at the same time every year? How does the weather affect the tree's processes? What other changes that might affect the tree(s) have taken place?

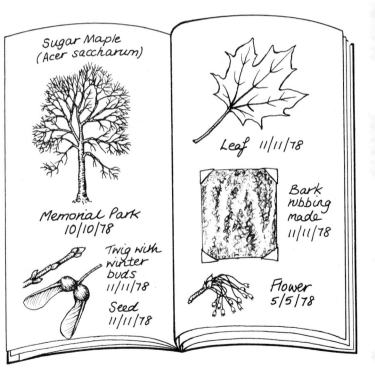

Sugar Maple
(*Acer saccharum*)

Memorial Park
10/10/78

Twig with winter buds
11/11/78

Seed
11/11/78

Leaf 11/11/78

Bark rubbing made
11/11/78

Flower
5/5/78

Books to read

A Guide to Field Identification; Trees of North America. C. Frank Brockman and Rebecca Merrilees. A Golden Press paperback with color pictures and range maps.

Master Tree Finder. May T. Watts. A small paperback published by the Nature Study Guild. Covers everything east of the Rocky Mountains. Identifies trees by their leaves. A handy pocket guide.

Desert Tree Finder. May T. Watts and Tom Watts. Same format as the *Master Tree Finder.* This guide covers southwestern California, Arizona, and New Mexico.

A Field Guide to Trees and Shrubs. George Petrides. A paperback in the Peterson Field Guide series, published by Houghton Mifflin, Co. Covers northeastern and central North America.

Trees of our National Forests; Their Beauty and Use. U.S. Department of Agriculture. An informative booklet about the National Forests and the major trees found in them.

International Book of Trees. Hugh Johnson. A large hardcover book with color photographs, published by Simon and Schuster. Worth getting out of the library.

Places to visit

Petrified Forest National Park, Arizona.

Joshua Tree National Monument, Twenty-nine Palms, California.

Muir Woods National Monument, Mill Valley, California.

Sequoia National Park, Three Rivers, California.

University of California Botanical Gardens, Berkeley, California.

U.S. National Arboretum, Washington, D.C.

Everglades National Park, Homestead, Florida.

Fairchild Tropical Gardens, Miami, Florida.

Chicago Natural History Museum, Chicago, Illinois.

Morton Arboretum, Lisle, Illinois.

Huntington Arboretum, Muncie, Indiana.

Huntingdon Garden, Los Angeles, California.

Lilly Cornett Woods, Skyline, Kentucky.

Arnold Arboretum, Jamaica Plain (Boston), Massachusetts.

American Museum of Natural History, New York, New York.

Bronx Botanical Gardens, Bronx, New York.

Brooklyn Botanical Gardens, Brooklyn, New York.

Planting Fields Arboretum, Oyster Bay, New York.

Joyce Kilmer Memorial Forest, Robbinsville, North Carolina.

Sara P. Duke Gardens, Durham, North Carolina.

Dysart Woods, Belmont, Ohio.

Longwood Gardens, Kennett Square, Pennsylvania.

Cypress Gardens, Magnolia Gardens, Middleton Place Gardens–all near Charleston, South Carolina.

Great Smoky Mountain National Park, Gatlinburg, Tennessee.

Wind River Experimental Forest, Vancouver, Washington.

Madison Arboretum, Madison, Wisconsin.

Trees for Tomorrow Camp, Eagle River, Wisconsin.

Scorecard

When you have seen and identified a tree, use this scorecard to look up the number of points you have scored.

Before looking up your score, look at the map below to find out which area you have seen the tree in. You will see that North America has been divided into five different areas: Northeast, Southeast, Central, Northwest and Southwest. There is a separate scorecard for each of these areas, and the trees that can be found in each area have been listed in alphabetical order.

A low score (the lowest is 5) means that the tree is common and quite easy to find; the highest score is 25, and the higher the score the rarer the tree in that area.

For instance, the Red Maple is fairly common in the North and Southeast (scores 5), rare in the Central and Northwest areas (scores 25), and not found at all in the Southwest.

When you have found your score, you can either ring it in pencil in the book, or you can keep a record of your score in a notebook, making a note of the date you see the flower. Either way you can add up your total score whenever you like – at the end of each day, week or month.

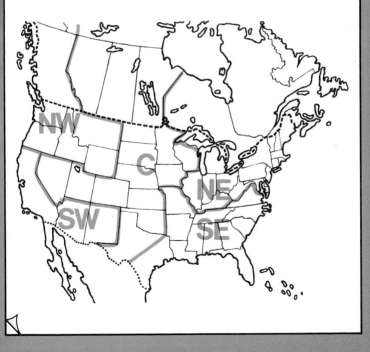

Northeast

This area includes the following states and provinces: Connecticut, Delaware, Illinois, Indiana, Kentucky, Maine, Maryland, Massachusetts, Michigan, New Brunswick, New Hampshire, New Jersey, New York, Newfoundland, Nova Scotia, Ohio, Ontario, Pennsylvania, Quebec, Rhode Island, Vermont, West Virginia.

	Score		Score		Score
Ash, White	10	Fir, Balsam	10	Oak, Willow	25
Aspen, Quaking	10	Ginkgo	10	Pagoda Tree	20
Beech, American	10	Gum, Sweet	15	Pine, Austrian	5
Beech, Purple	20	Hemlock, Eastern	10	Pine, Jeffrey	25
Birch, Paper	10	Hickory, Shagbark	10	Pine, Ponderosa	25
Birch, European White	20	Linden, American	5	Pine, Scots	5
Birch, Swedish	25	Linden, Small-leafed	10	Pine, White	5
Bitternut	20	Maple, Norway	5	Poplar, Balsam	10
Buttonwood	10	Maple, Red	5	Poplar, Lombardy	5
Catalpa	20	Maple, Silver	5	Redwood, Dawn	20
Cedar, Western Red	25	Maple, Sugar	5	Sassafras	20
Cherry, Sweet	20	Mimosa	10	Spruce, Blue Colorado	10
Chestnut, Horse	5	Mulberry, White	20	Spruce, Norway	5
Cottonwood	5	Oak, Burr	15	Tamarack	15
Cypress, Swamp	20	Oak, Pin	15	Tree of Heaven	20
Deodar	25	Oak, Post	25	Tulip Tree	15
Elm, American	5	Oak, Red	5	Walnut, Black	10
Empress Tree	25	Oak, White	10	Willow, Weeping	10

Southeast

This area includes the following states:
Alabama, Arkansas, Florida, Georgia, Louisiana, Mississippi, Missouri, North Carolina, South Carolina, Tennessee, Texas (eastern), Virginia

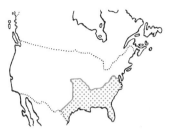

	Score		Score		Score
Ash, White	20	Locust, Black	15	Palmetto, Cabbage	20
Beech, American	5	Locust, Honey	5	Pear, Bradford	20
Buttonwood	5	Magnolia, Southern	5	Pecan	5
Catalpa, Southern	10	Maple, Norway	20	Pine, Loblolly	5
Chestnut, Horse	25	Maple, Red	5	Pine, White	10
Cottonwood	5	Maple, Silver	15	Poplar, Lombardy	5
Cypress, Italian	15	Maple, Sugar	15	Redwood, Dawn	20
Cypress, Swamp	10	Mimosa	5	Sassafras	10
Deodar	10	Mulberry, White	20	Spruce, Blue Colorado	15
Elm, American	5	Oak, Blackjack	5	Spruce, Norway	5
Elm, Siberian	25	Oak, Burr	20	Sugarberry	10
Empress Tree	20	Oak, Live	10	Tallow Tree, Chinese	15
Ginkgo	10	Oak, Pin	10	Tree of Heaven	5
Gum, Sweet	5	Oak, Post	5	Tulip Tree	5
Hemlock, Eastern	10	Oak, Red	15	Walnut, Black	10
Hickory, Shagbark	25	Oak, White	5	Washingtonia, California	25
Linden, American	20	Oak, Willow	5	Washingtonia, Mexican	20
Linden, Small-leafed	25	Palm, Canary	20	Willow, Babylon	10

Central

This area includes the following states and provinces:
Alberta, Colorado, Iowa, Kansas, Manitoba, Minnesota, Nebraska, Nevada, North Dakota, Oklahoma, Saskatchewan, South Dakota, Texas (western), Utah, Wisconsin

	Score		Score		Score
Aspen, Quaking	5	Locust, Honey	5	Pine, Limber	15
Beech, Purple	25	Magnolia, Southern	25	Pine, Lodgepole	10
Birch, Paper	20	Maple, Norway	20	Pine, Ponderosa	10
Birch, European White	10	Maple, Red	25	Pine, Scots	15
Birch, Swedish	5	Maple, Silver	10	Pine, White	15
Buttonwood	15	Maple, Sugar	15	Poplar, Balsam	10
Catalpa	20	Mimosa	20	Poplar, Bolle's	10
Chestnut, Horse	5	Mulberry, White	20	Poplar, Lombardy	5
Cottonwood	5	Oak, Blackjack	20	Sassafras	20
Cypress, Swamp	25	Oak, Burr	10	Spruce, Colorado	5
Elm, American	5	Oak, Pin	10	Spruce, Engelmann	10
Elm, Siberian	5	Oak, Post	20	Spruce, Norway	15
Ginkgo	20	Oak, Red	10	Sugarberry	10
Gum, Sweet	20	Oak, White	15	Tamarack	20
Hickory, Shagbark	25	Olive, Russian	15	Tree of Heaven	15
Linden, American	15	Pagoda Tree	25	Walnut, Black	15
Linden, Small-leafed	10	Pear, Bradford	25	Willow, Weeping	10
Locust, Black	20	Pine, Austrian	5		

Northwest

This area includes the following
states and provinces:
British Columbia, Idaho, Montana,
Oregon, Washington, Wyoming

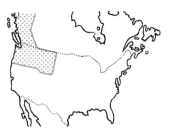

	Score		Score		Score
Aspen, Quaking	15	Hemlock, Western	5	Pine, Ponderosa	5
Ash, White	15	Linden, American	25	Pine, Scots	20
Beech, American	25	Linden, Small-leafed	15	Poplar, Balsam	5
Beech, Purple	20	Locust, Black	5	Poplar, Lombardy	5
Birch, Paper	15	Locust, Honey	10	Redwood, Coast	25
Birch, European White	10	Maple, Norway	20	Redwood, Dawn	25
Birch, Swedish	10	Maple, Oregon	5	Sequoia, Giant	20
Catalpa	20	Maple, Red	25	Spruce, Colorado	10
Cedar, Western Red	5	Maple, Silver	15	Spruce, Engelmann	15
Cherry, Sweet	10	Maple, Sugar	25	Spruce, Norway	15
Chestnut, Horse	5	Mulberry, White	25	Spruce, Sitka	10
Deodar	15	Oak, Pin	20	Sugarberry	15
Elm, American	20	Oak, Red	25	Tree of Heaven	15
Elm, Siberian	25	Pagoda Tree	25	Tulip Tree	20
Empress Tree	25	Pine, Austrian	20	Walnut, Black	25
Fir, Douglas	5	Pine, Jeffrey	20	Willow, Weeping	10
Ginkgo	25	Pine, Limber	25		
Gum, Sweet	15	Pine, Lodgepole	10		

Southwest

This area includes the following states:
Arizona, California, New Mexico

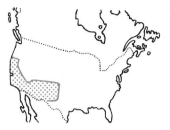

	Score		Score		Score
Aspen, Quaking	20	Olive, Russian	10	Tree of Heaven	10
Birch, European White	5	Palm, Canary	5	Tulip Tree	25
Catalpa, Southern	15	Palmetto, Cabbage	5	Washingtonia, California	5
Cypress, Italian	10	Pine, Aleppo	10	Washingtonia, Mexican	5
Deodar	5	Pine, Canary	10		
Elm, Siberian	5	Pine, Jeffrey	15		
Empress Tree	20	Pine, Limber	25		
Fir, Douglas	15	Pine, Lodgepole	15		
Ginkgo	25	Pine, Ponderosa	5		
Gum, Blue	5	Poplars, Balsam	20		
Gum, Sweet	15	Poplar, Bolle's	20		
Hemlock, Western	20	Poplar, Lombardy	5		
Locust, Black	15	Redwood, Coast	10		
Locust, Honey	10	Redwood, Dawn	20		
Magnolia, Southern	10	Sequoia, Giant	20		
Maple, Silver	15	Spruce, Colorado	10		
Mulberry, White	20	Spruce, Sitka	25		
Nut Pine, Single-leaf	20	Tallow Tree, Chinese	15		

Index

If a tree has another common name which is also widely used, this is shown below in parentheses. On the next page you will find a list of the Latin names of the trees, since, though the common name may vary from one part of the country to another, the Latin name remains the same.

Index of Latin names